GRAVITY
FOR
SMARTYPANTS

Anushka Ravishankar

ILLUSTRATED BY
Pia Alizé Hazarika

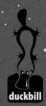

duckbill

An imprint of Penguin Random House

DUCKBILL BOOKS

USA | Canada | UK | Ireland | Australia
New Zealand | India | South Africa | China

Duckbill Books is part of the Penguin Random House group of companies
whose addresses can be found at global.penguinrandomhouse.com

Published by Penguin Random House India Pvt. Ltd
4th Floor, Capital Tower 1, MG Road,
Gurugram 122 002, Haryana, India

Penguin
Random House
India

First published in Duckbill Books by
Penguin Random House India 2022

10 9 8 7 6 5 4 3 2 1

ISBN 9780143454106

Typeset in ArcherPro by DiTech Publishing Services Pvt. Ltd
Printed at Aarvee Promotions, India

www.penguin.co.in

NEWTON'S LAW OF GRAVITATION

Any two bodies attract each other with a force that is proportional to the product of their two masses and inversely proportional to the square of the distance between them.

Things fall.

This is because of **gravity**.

If you jump, you fall downwards.

This is also because of gravity. Gravity pulls things down.

Things stay on the ground.

This is because
of gravity too.

Gravity pulls everything down.

You want to know
what gravity is?
First, you need to
know what matter is.

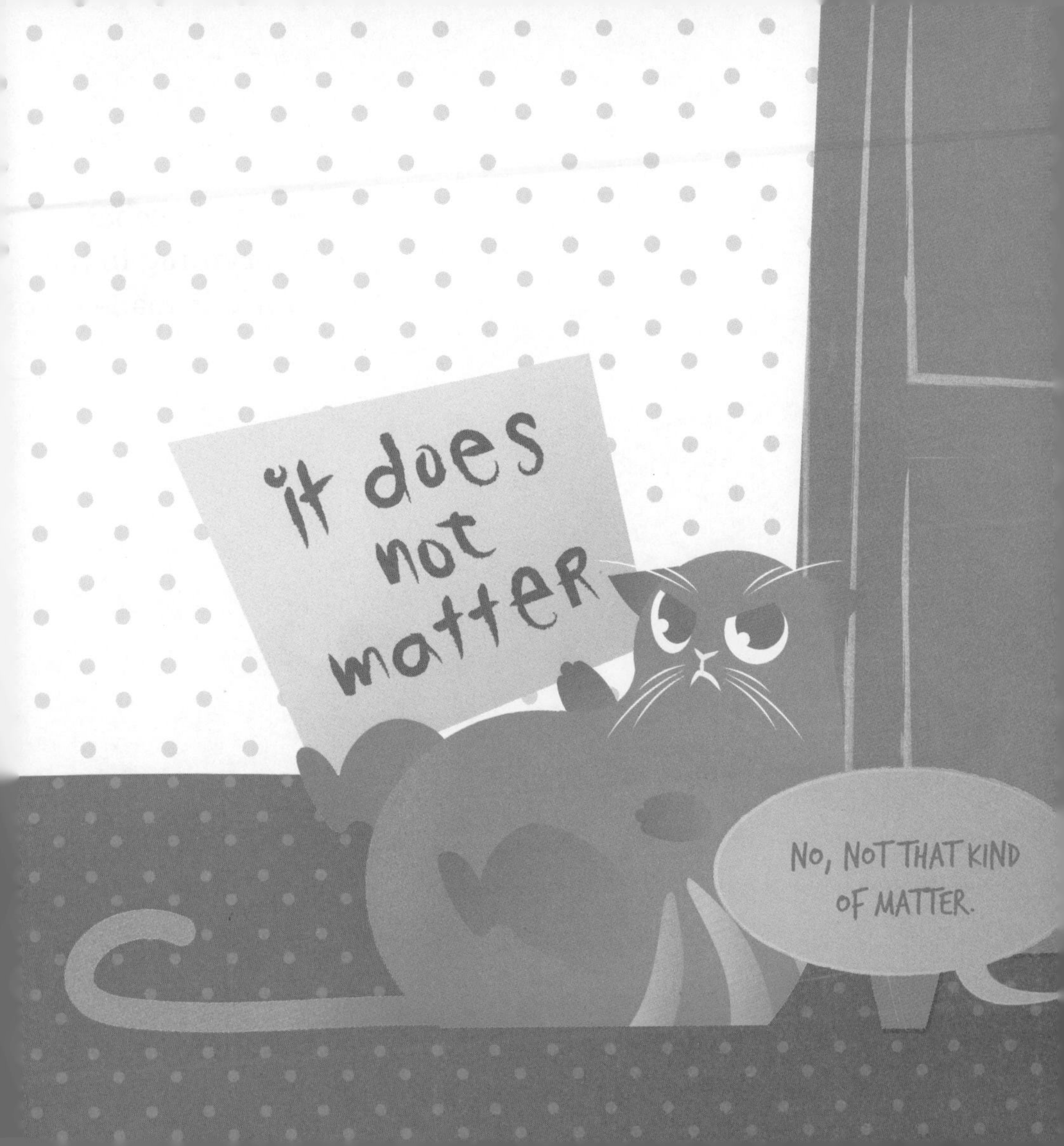
it does not matter
No, NOT THAT KIND OF MATTER.

Matter is what
everything in the
world is made up of

Things that have
matter have **mass**.

Things with more
matter have more mass.

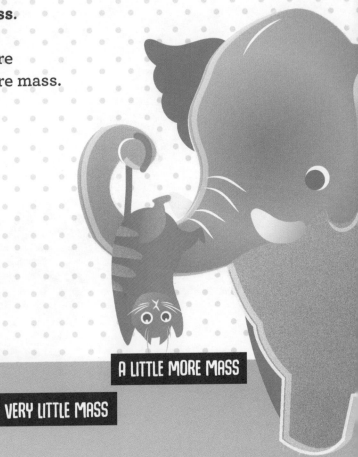

A LITTLE MORE MASS

VERY LITTLE MASS

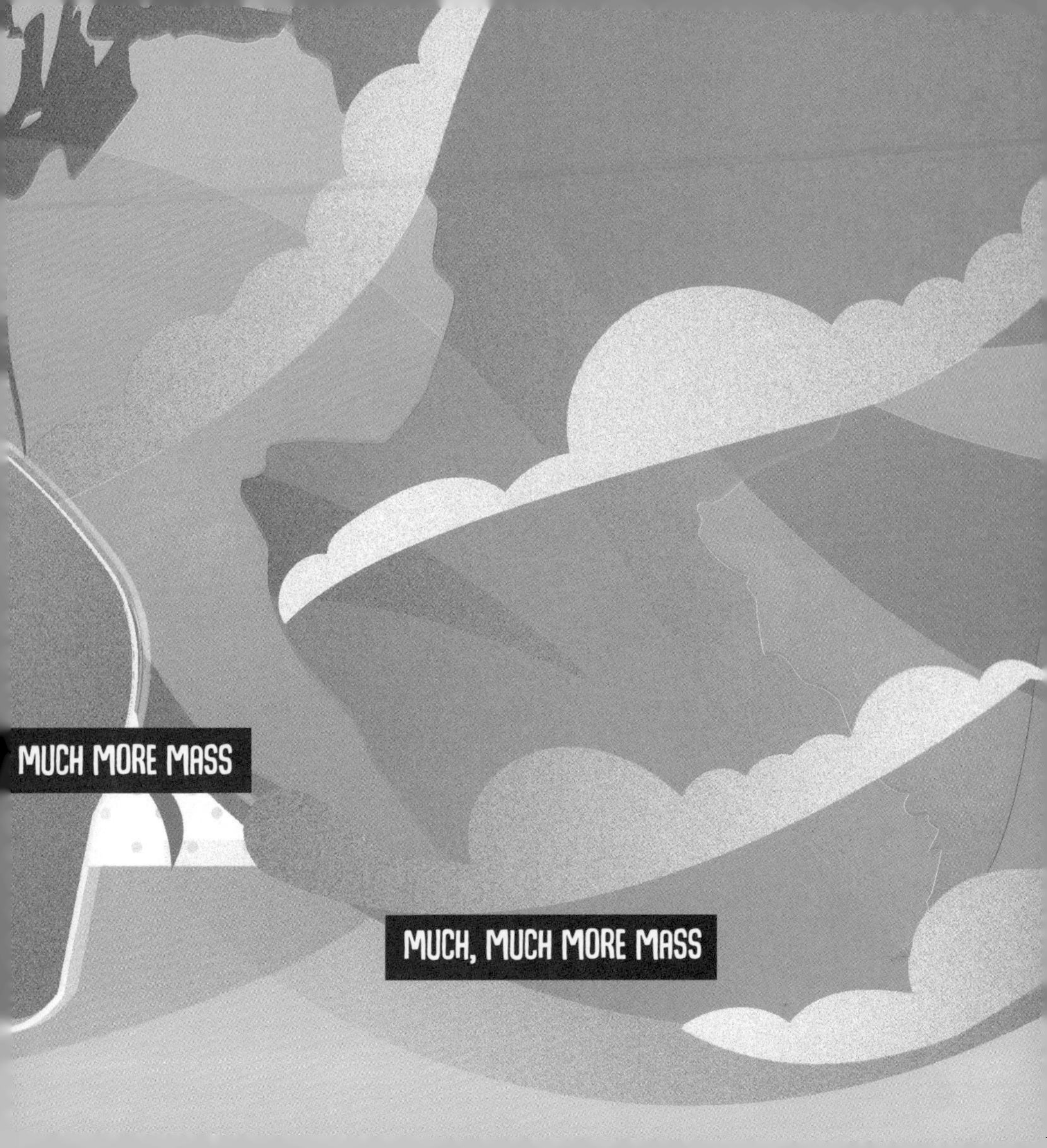
MUCH MORE MASS
MUCH, MUCH MORE MASS

The Earth has **SO** much mass that you can't even imagine it.

THAT'S TRUE. I DON'T KNOW HOW MUCH YOU CAN IMAGINE.
MAYBE YOU CAN.
ALL RIGHT, YOU CAN.
I SAID OKAY!

Two things with mass pull each other. This pull, which is also called **force**, is gravity.

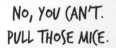

The pull or gravity of a thing
is more if its mass is more.

CRUNCH
CRUNCH
CRUNCH

The Earth has so much mass that the gravity of the planet pulls everything towards it.

That's why things fall down.

If Earth had no gravity,
we would all fly off from its
surface and float in space.

YES, THAT WOULD BE FUN, BUT YOU MIGHT GET HUNGRY.
NO, I WOULDN'T BE ABLE TO FEED YOU IN SPACE.

The sun has much more mass than the Earth.

Gravity makes the Earth go around the sun.

Bzzzzzzzzzzt
No, THE FLY IS NOT BEING PULLED BY YOUR GRAVITY.
IT'S JUST FLYING AROUND YOUR HEAD.

The moon has less mass than the Earth.

Gravity makes the moon
go round the Earth.

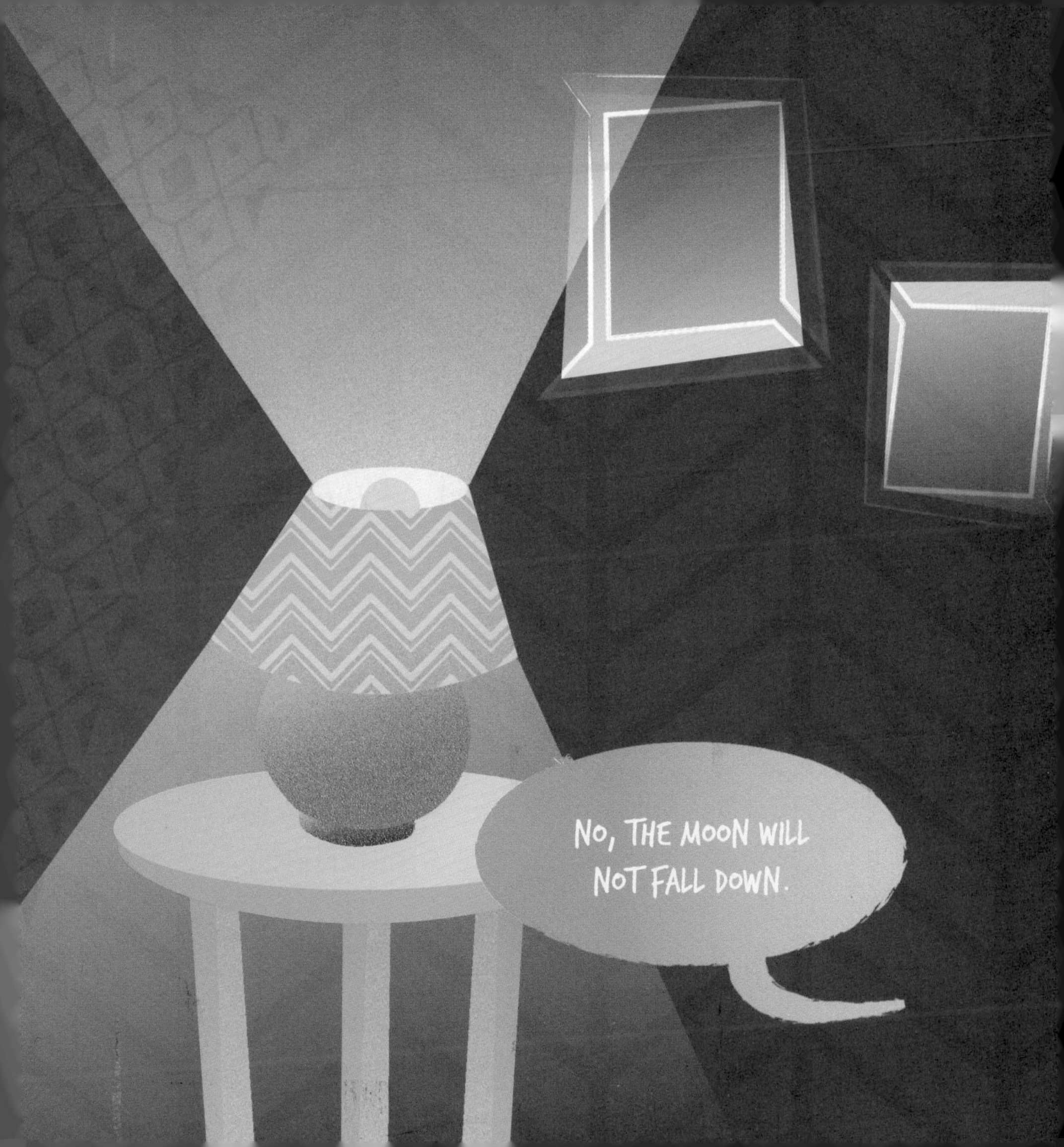
NO, THE MOON WILL NOT FALL DOWN.

YOU CAN HIDE IF YOU WANT TO, BUT THE MOON IS NOT GOING TO FALL DOWN.
OKAY, YOU CAN SLEEP THERE.

THAT'S TRUE, YOU WILL STAY THERE BECAUSE OF THE EARTH'S GRAVITY.
NO, I'M NOT GOING TO DROP ANY TREATS.
YES IF I DID, THEY WOULD FALL DOWN BECAUSE OF GRAVITY.
YES, SMARTYPANTS, YOU KNOW ALL ABOUT GRAVITY NOW.

Anushka Ravishankar likes
science, cats and books, not
necessarily in that order. So
she decided to write a book to
explain science to a cat. The cat
doesn't always get the point,
but she hopes her readers will.

Pia Alizé Hazarika is an illustrator primarily interested in comics and visual narratives.

Her independent/collaborative work has been published by Penguin Random House India (*The PAO Anthology*), COMIX INDIA, Manta Ray Comics, The Pulpocracy, Captain Bijli Comics, Yoda Press, Zubaan Books and the Khoj Artists Collective. She runs PIG Studio, an illustration-driven space, based out of New Delhi.

Her handle on Instagram is @_PigStudio_